thank you for believing
in me
thank you for reading
♡

2021

poetry & script by mackenzie akin
cover & illustrations by almy bartis

doodle, star a page, write in the margins, underline words, circle things... mark these pages in whatever ways are meaningful to you. i included a few blank pages, if you would like to jot down thoughts, feelings or memories that come to mind.

table of contents

poetry	...1-139
lists for perspective	...143-149
behind the poems	...151-171
acknowledgments	...173
about the author	...175
q+a with the author	...178-181
copyright information	...183
sneak peek at volume two	...185-189

valleys in my mind

there are valleys in my mind
reflecting streams
      little tents
            old lanterns
                  young hearts
enough light from the moon
and stars
you wouldn't believe
letting me see the soft cotton
layered
on
your
shoulder
and your eyes traveling over
as if it's the
sweetest
adventure
you have ever known.

the thought of you
y o u
i became tired
so softly.
retracing the pattern
calloused hands
on the peak of lace
how could i forget?

years believing
that all i could do
is watch her
be beautiful
and different

wanting
to capture your eye
your heart
your hopes

a dream
a work of art

not knowing
i was already a masterpiece
in progress.

there are moments
i wish i could experience
a thousand lives,
love,
and adventure.
pluck a favorite from the reel,
bask in that time.

some irony,
being a writer-
books and movies are the closest
the closest
to that wish.

nothing i crave more
than my words
my mind
bound
for the world to read
to let my creative heart
rise above my doubts

and here i am
doing everything i once dreamed.

so sweet
my love
so *sweet*
spinning softly in time

finding me
like broken pieces
to your favorite record.

draw me from the shelf
spin me once through
honey
i can do whatever you need me to.

i'll carry you from the shadows
to where the light streams in

i'll save you from the waves
the storms
you just have to let me in.

valleys in my mind 7

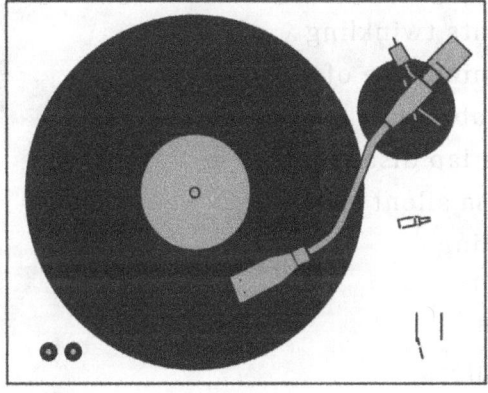

all i see
lights twinkling
reminds me of a dream
a cabin on a lake of black glass
the lap disappears
from silent snow
falling
still
and
endless
i b r e a t h e.

curling up with a book has got to be
the best feeling

it's an experience
you cry
you dream
a secret life between your hands

face it,
you desire to be drawn by Her pen.

if it had to be
you and me,
what would you say?

if it had to be
you and me,
would the skies bleed pink
or gray?

my mind feels like the rain
drown it all away

hope for my heart
but
pleasure in the pain.

will i ever forget the rage,
the promises erased?
thought you would be there
but you were never meant to stay.

13

what's wrong with them this time?

oh,
that part of their brain
the one that deals with
emotion
l o g i c
it hasn't fully developed yet.

they see the world
as a product of their love
it's not anywhere close
to what they need.

they burn
e v e r y t h i n g.

when all else fails

r e a d.

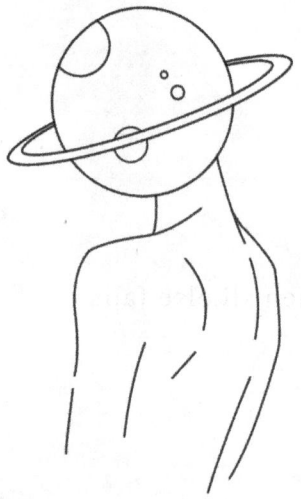

i don't know how to exist
in the world that you do.

"you're gone" i mutter, turning the corner
forcing breath through the doors
with something that i hadn't felt for years.

i don't go down that hall anymore
no peace,
no support,
no warmth,
like there once was.

the way you spoke to me,
as if i held the world
at my fingertips.
as if it would never
end like this.

i wish i could sit right
there.
ask you a million questions of life
how you always knew
but
you are just utterly committed to ash,
wind wisping at what once was.
all i could ever want
haunting my memories.

you were there,
but there's no going back.

optimism
doing the right thing
imagine
a world
like
that.

hey
today
in history
they needed you.

i stepped in
like so many times before
before
but i can't find a way
to change all that i thought
about you.

today
in history
i needed you.

i stepped out
for the first time
after.
i knew i would not try,
as history
would not repeat itself.

wildflowers
oh, how they dance
whitman
   navy shutters
      sinking sun
         second chances.

there's a lesson in every mistake
there's a lesson in every breakdown
speak to your scattered pieces
speak to your traumas
speak to your jealousy
speak to your bitterness
accept that you may not receive closure
accept yourself as a healing
imperfect being
everything
everything
is temporary
will change
and grow.

when you ask me
if i'm okay,
i say
yes.

you think that you know me.
yes
to be understood
is a girl's dream
but you cannot claim to know me
without seeing what i've been through
without seeing my mind in disarray
without feeling the rivers of joy
flowing free most days
otherwise trickling over an abyss

when you ask me
if i'm okay,
i write to tell you
no.

i think collateral damage
comes from wanting people
to hurt for me too.

reflections

some days i am attached,
together;
other days bring fire.

although i don't understand my mind
she holds me
as if she needs me.
although she drags me under
where would i be without her?
although her thoughts etch bullet wounds
although she bullies
and bullies.

although i don't like how i feel
although i don't like what i see
i love her
still.

suggested writing prompt: what are two things you wish were different about you? do you have days that "bring fire"... what influences those days, adds fuel to the fire?

*suggested prompt: what is it about you, that you love?
name three things you are proud of yourself for.*

my mind is hyperventilating
screaming
but my body is still
i don't say anything
i won't say anything.

i'm sorry you've been hurt
i'm sorry you've been broken
there can be beauty in that pain
but for now,
share your truth.

i'm sorry they don't see your worth
by "they" i might mean "you"
but i'm here
even when no one else will
i'll care for you.

i didn't know when i would be ready
to say all that i have to
i pulled the blinds one morning
thought of my heart
poured some coffee
and knew it was time to fucking roll with it.

some people can be saved
and
everyone is worth saving.

her spot

sometimes she is sitting at the bridge
knees folded in close
water twirling beneath her
bends
dances
like a whisper from a lost friend.

she cut again
her hair
she sits so alone
breathing in the night

peepers calling into field pockets
peering over
just shades of black
but it's kinda beautiful

she wishes she could float down the creek
through the dips and under the trees

she doesn't know why she comes here
other than the fact that being in this spot
her spot
makes her feel alive.

i guess she feels like she is dying.

valleys in my mind **33**

suggested writing prompt: what makes you feel alive?

reading, writing, nature
fill my soul with joy
they give me the space to dream
it's quiet
it's freedom
it's all i've ever wanted.

there hasn't been a time where i felt
so connected to a series,
as i do with Throne of Glass.
but it has my heart
and its complexity
is forever worth my praise.

i want to find my carranam.

[inspired by Throne of Glass by Sarah J. Maas]

it angers me
to hear what you have been through
the lies
the manipulation
cheating.

if it's anything like my journey
they cheated
long before
before that single instance you discovered

and

i don't want to be a n y t h i n g like her.

care and love
are so different.

my love was like a well,
pieces of us seemed to fill it
but echoed at the bottom.

my love was like a well,
and you drank
til it
ran dry.

valleys in my mind 41

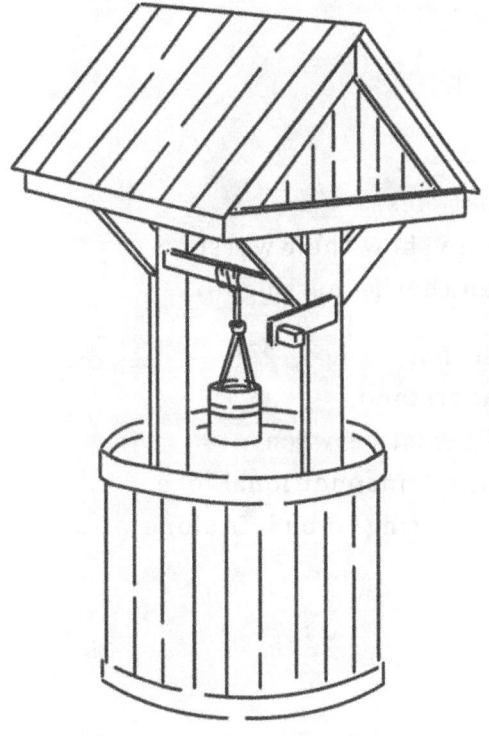

sometimes,
people show their worst
when they're hurting.

with that,
i understand
i will exist between
wanting unconditional love
and wanting to be left alone.

i think of my father
the times he and the Akin's
were happily lost
on sunday post-church back roads
a place known for its seamless spin with time.

it all comes full circle
we are an environmental mixture
defined by habits
love or lack of.
attachment anxiety
or
anxiety attachment.
how much we listen to the trees
how much we look at the sky
and pause.

if i can keep the mentality
of backroads in the seventies
i can keep my roots
replenish my heart.

drunk consent
is not consent

when you are drunk
you cannot consent

one consent
is not consent again

that trust you felt
he is not a friend

months and months
grey pain
coping by pushing away
and it's okay

carried higher
promises
too good to be you

my heart hasn't even been here
yet
reeling with demons
i can't forget

would you cherish me
adore me
if you knew me like that?

i can see myself–
a reflection in the sea,
blonde through the breeze,
a freckle or two.

maybe i felt complete.
i sat there,
and sat there.

did it hurt less back then?

i don't even know who i am anymore.

staying with sadness
is easier sometimes
than fighting
dragging myself
through the darkness.

is happiness stronger
when you've never felt your heart ache
or when you've experienced both
depression and peace
in their entirety?

my love,
i didn't want to go.

you'll find me in the snow
when it hugs the quiet pines

you'll find me in the wind
when it whispers with the leaves

you'll find me in the rain
when it kisses your soft skin

each day the sun fades
you'll find me
winter
    fall
        spring
i promise
i'll never leave you.

you are my world,

and i promise
you'll find me in yours.

50

questions without answers [yet]:

how did i become so consumed?

how did my life align like this?

will i ever completely accept my flaws?

will my heart ever feel full again?

will my children have freedom from my anxiety, or will it be instilled in them like breathing?

"just do it" he whispers.
"do what?"
"trust me."
"i don't know how to do that again.
to walk in, believing that you won't lie to me
or find someone else."

i enjoy alone time to be productive
but half the time i end up in bed,
suffocating thoughts with my blanket.

if i close my eyes,
maybe they'll stop tormenting me
reminding of failures and mistakes

wishing,
tears,
sabotage,
binge sadness-
i shrink in submission to my own mind.

why?

if it had to be
you and me,
i'd rather be lonely.

i'd rather be lonely.

he was a dream,
now a nightmare.

but this Hell that i can put him through
fists fly
chains quake
i growl-
i thought i w a s f r e e f r o m y o u.

behind me,
dormant recesses open.
you're closing in
a space never touched before
love
grace

you wrap around me
pulling me back from him
and i am suddenly
blanketed
in utter relief.
i am finally free from you.

                                    ^with some pieces, i sit back and
                                    question myself. where the heck
                                    did those words come from?

i don't remember me

i spent more time smiling...
no one had ever told me
that i looked tired.
don't you hate that?

but,
no one had ever asked me if i was okay.
why did it
why did y o u
have to come into my life?

what was it supposed to teach me?
nobody's perfect?
or
take care of my heart,
love wisely,
l o v e   m y s e l f   f i r s t,
after years of learning otherwise.

to the ones who don't understand us
we are more dirt road
to your four-lane world.

our minds race,
riled by pressure,
compassion,
apathy,
pulled identity-
an addiction,
cyclic obsession,
with escape.

we need to hold onto
each other.

451

the temperature in which words
stories
ignite
although it always
becomes much hotter
once it's burning.

[inspired by Fahrenheit 451 by Ray Bradbury]

i seem to always refer to flame
in my writing,
as if it is the only way to fathom
my immense feelings in this life.

i always thought that
i was more connected to water
than earth, wind,
or fire.
perhaps i have been grasping at
what i need most.

i think
i hated the reality
of what you had with them
because
i know how brokenly beautiful
your heart is.
how they cheated,
how much
you must have loved them,

opening your heart to them

and that i truly
have not done the same
until you.

there's something about
the way you looked at me.
pallets kindled,
your sweetness glowing with the
brisk air.
incessant.
consuming.
for the first time
in a long time,
i stopped thinking about
the world around me.

i was just
living
and i won't ever forget that.

we have only one night.
but i wonder,
is your heart filled
with hope
or misery?

if you could see the way i love,
you'd know that i'm all in.
what scares me is
you want me,
but for love
or for sin?

do you want to know my biggest dreams
and see me when i wake?
or are you chasing after lust
another soul to take?

but, you're with him

jaded,
your eyes have never been so beautiful.
jaded,
your eyes have never been
so bright,
hopeful,
but jaded.

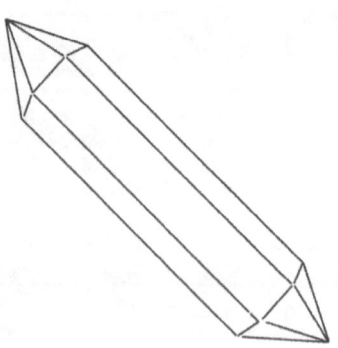

you must have been so lonely too.

each day that i push forward,
is a day farther from pain.

each day that i push forward,
is a day farther from pain.

these eyes i'm staring into
touch
hypnotizing
he grabs what i wish was his.

my kiss,
learning this,
i won't let him go

and he'll never know.

relationships take
e v e r y t h i n g.
you can be guarded
smart
but you'll still let them in
or you'll let them *back in*.

"why should i ever try again"

but
the moments i now regret
built my i d e n t i t y.
i'm stronger
whether i believe it or not.

i couldn't imagine you raising our children,
i saw your mind close even more.

the love songs weren't about you anymore.
i'm sorry.

no, i'm not sorry.
you didn't care about me.
you used me.
i dodged a bullet.

there's something about Fate.

when i imagined my future
lying quietly on my bed
i never saw you,
but She did.

how did She decide?
when looking at you
if She felt
even half of what i do,
she must have whispered
"twenty-twenty"
with a smirk.

breathing a chapter into existence
some pages torn out
a new title
signed and stamped,
"a love without an ending."

there's quite a peace to be gathered
looking back at my writing
sinking into the creative moments
to articulate my imagination,
a wonderful mess of an imagination.

sometimes i will just change a line,
or a word,
and smile because *i can do that*
it's all mine.

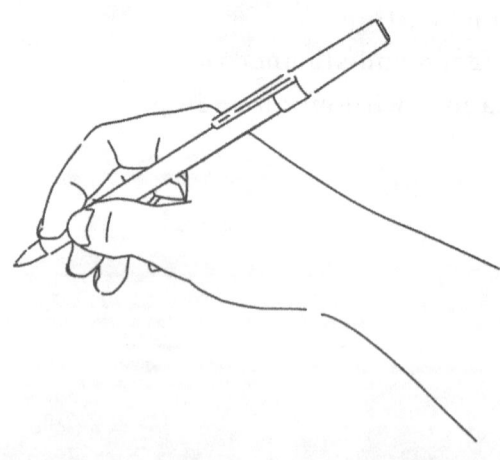

some days
i remember
i try to tell myself,
that he broke me
broke.
me.
but i still open up
i let the sun in
blankets wrapped for a minute
and allow happy thoughts
to hold me.
was it all destructive?
was it all poison to my soul?

wanting
you
will

never

e n d.

my heart and mind tell different stories
one's an author
one's an artist.

i picture my heart tucked into a studio
unphased
creating what she desires
with bright colors and warmth
but letting the landlord collect
bully
demolish her masterpieces
with a single thought

i can reach out to my mind
on the moon
but it's too far and
you can only see the light side.

He lifts her up
off the sheets
in a breathless daze,
and carries her to the glass
where she can see the art
of the skies and fields.
she wants to dream again.

someday
the pain
lessons
waiting
aching
longing
will all make sense.

if i said the first thought
rushing my mind
i'd be single
i'd be broken
even more than i imagined.
i'd burn
everything around me.

my subconscious doesn't play fair.
a sadist,
she ignites trust,
tears at self-image
d o e s n o t c a r e.

can i blame her?
she's a product of my experiences
how i chose to internalize
how i force it into her lap
out of sight, out of mind
she learned how to survive.

"you write so beautifully, the inside of your mind must be a terrible place" i once read.

yes, but it is so special.
my enemy some days,
my biggest fan...
just a touch of anxiety though.
regret
optimism
sabotage
wonder
resiliency
shall i continue?

suggested writing prompt: what makes your mind beautiful? or, how can it become a more positive space?

I can call it growth,
standing still
is trouble
sometimes
sometimes
                        ...
it's not growth,
it's escaping

i can't call it growth.
standing still
same people
    same goals
        same blame
            same pain
it's not growth
it's deception.

what day
is the literal day
that i will lose my mind?
i go out,
come back,
waves won't stop
rolling over sand.
each time i wonder,
when will i not return?

will i feel free?

promises,
lost track.
lies,
lost track.

i realized,
the sun never rose for me
for us.

was anything real?
give me back time.
i should've known
i should've known
you were never mine.

you hold pieces of me
still

g i v e

t h e m

b a c k.

years wondering
does unconditional love exist?

or am i forever bound as a lesson
for boys not yet men
repressed emotions
lack of intention
patterned paranoia
worth at his whim

i sink into the places we used to be.

staring at my phone,
thinking you felt the same.
but what parts of that night
didn't spark a flame?

run, sweet girl, run

if he has the power to hurt you,
step back.
and if he has the power to *break* you
run.
please run.
with time, i promise
you will never
never
regret it.

leave a message [please]
hey,
i don't expect you to forgive me.
i'm truly sorry.
you sacrificed everything for me.
i wasted your time.
i want to make things right.
i wish i could go back and change
    what i said.
    what i did.
i didn't deserve you.
i don't forgive myself.

-k.e.n.

suggested prompt: imagine someone who hurt you, left you a voicemail. what do you wish they would say to you?

i am alive.
i don't know if it's the churning in my gut,
salt in the air,
or sun on my skin,
but The Notebook always makes me feel
this way-
such bliss and quarrel.
memories
wishing

longing

lap on the rocks.

i don't think
i could ever not care,
but now i know
i need to learn
to delegate my power.
don't give my power to comparison.
don't give power to trauma.
don't give power to arguments.
don't give my power to men
    who aren't in my kingdom anymore.

i started to feel lonely in the relationship.
that's when i knew it was time to move on.

drowning

someone expressed
mental health
mental illness
on a spectrum.
it's a continuum
rather than existing within borders.

i knew i could make it there,
i could swim to the shore,
instead of drowning
in you.

past lives

i think of those out of body moments
like another soul is dancing inside me.
only my spirit can feel it
wind through my hair
bareback
wild.

what am i supposed to experience
in this life
that i didn't in the last?

suggested topic: what do you imagine in your past life?

dear little girl,

trying to show the world
what you are made of
trying to forget
what hurt you.
and tears
that pushed fear and
you stare at the mirror,
trying to see something other than yourself
but it will be okay.
from this season,
you will be stronger than you were.
start with your goals
chase them.
buy the bright cleats,
tie up your hair, add the eye black.
find a soccer ball that makes you light up,
give that soccer ball a name of its own,
Florence,
Dean.
get into the huddle,
take a deep breath,
take to the field,
take to the rain,
take to the enemy,
stand tall-
we are one and the same.

check out "behind the poems" to learn why "dear little girl" was written.

suggested writing prompt: what would you say to your younger self?

a love letter to myself

i didn't know
how to fix you.
i didn't know
that we would be hurting like this.

i didn't understand you
and how some days you feel growth,
and love
in your bones.
and how some days you feel destruction,
and aching
through everything.

i didn't understand you
until i chose to *try*
every day,
every damn day
to be better,
kinder
to you.

i hope you know,
i will fight for you
always.

suggested prompt: what would you write in a love letter to yourself?

though i'm driving,
my eyes are everywhere.
thoughts colliding
like wind-blown pines.

i'm in the past.
i know you are too.

i once considered the past a reflection,
a compass toward growth.
but i need to confess,
my past is only a distraction.
it's toxic.

i keep draining myself
by living in the past
and i am miles,
miles away,
from where i want to be.

growth comes from change
set on action,
not regret.

learn from the past,
then move on.

move
on.

i like how my time can be spent
on anything,
literally anything,
and i don't w a s t e it
on y o u.

if he ever lied to you,
you know the answer.
if you ever cried yourself to sleep over him,
you know the answer.

if you wonder if he is "the one,"
you already know the answer.

selfishness,
it's all that i can ask of myself.
stay present,
stay steady.

though i didn't see it at the time,
becoming single
was the biggest form
of self-love
i could've ever given myself.

i needed to be here
for myself
and nobody else.

i want to teach you self-love
no
i want you to inherently love yourself
above all else.
but i fear self-love
is only a product
of days turning into nights,
of failed relationships,
unresolved heartache
cheating,
comparison,
wondering why-
why would he leave me?

we all want time
more time
replay the good memories,
change the past
but life races on.

we want to change ourselves
and we can
but it requires our time to do that.
nothing worthwhile is quick.
everything worth investing in
is long-term.

it takes time
to heal
to feel better
to feel anything
to pick up the pieces of our former selves
and it's okay.

i cannot be perfect.
i will never be.
perfection does not exist.

the people we wish we could be?
the people we wish we could look like?
you don't see their broken parts.
you don't see their sleepless nights.
you don't know how many tears they've cried
over stupid guys,
or heartless women,
trauma,
uncertainty.

you cannot be perfect,
you never will be,

but i will be better each day.
you can be better each day.

take a day to shut down.
don't consider it a step backward.

even the greatest queens
learn their strengths and weaknesses,
overwhelmed
by the silent wars waging
in a dusk-lit mind chamber.

taking a break
is evidence that you are listening
to your needs.
that is a step forward.

suggested writing prompt: if you could have a day off, to yourself, what would it look like?

when you are a writer,
    you never die.
put it to paper,
collapse,
coffee,
repeat.
without writing,
you're coasting
on a level quite like suffocation
and not knowing who you are.

when you love a writer,
    you never die.
your story doesn't fade
after the heartache;
you become someone else.
page by page,
your story is laced
into the grand journey of my heart.

when you love a writer,
    who are you?
the rock
her rock
or the knife?
your very existence is heavy
i press the tip so boldly
it breaks.

when you find a writer,
>   you never die.
their story hugs your own
and you know you're not in it alone.
they give breath
a heartbeat
to your pain.

artists never die.

i find it easier
to breathe lust
into loneliness
than to
learn how to love.

easier
to fall
than how you
left.

easier
to recover from the rain
than survive
a flame.

easier
to love you
than to learn
to love myself.

easier
to

valleys in my mind 119

restlessness is your sign.

healing,
true healing,
is grieving-
releasing memories
though you came to
identify
with the pain.

my markers of beauty:

your smile
eyes that tell stories
kindness to strangers
vulnerability
the courage that dances with it
seeking brightness in the darkness
learning
letting go.

think of
what love can be,
what you want love to be.
chase that.

i didn't get where i am today
with delightful chapters.
pages were soaked with tears,
over half the book is insecurity.

but if the book of my life was just anxiety
and doubt
the protagonist could never be happy.

i have been pushed into a change
that consisted of recognizing my flaws.
i was angry,
i was selfish,
i was emotional,
i was mean.
i lied,
and i sat quietly as my own mind
tore me apart.

but now i take each day
as a day to be kind to myself-
to breathe.
i know that i deserve the best
and all i'm trying to say
is have hope.
and fight hard for your happy ending.

you write this life.

suggested writing prompt: the chapters of your life, what would they look like? how are you moving forward from this journey in a more positive light?

i used to wonder
how you could throw your life away.
holding onto the pain
tight to your chest,
as if it's the only thing
making you feel alive.

now,
i get it.

you aren't throwing your life away.
you watch it
loudly
fall through your fingers like sand.

now,
i get it.

just know
i had to s a v e myself.

"he broke me."
i cling to his shirt "h e   b r o k e   m e."

"but i'm not him.
i'm not him.
don't let these thoughts
take you away from me.
please."

sharing our feelings,
is the most conflicting experience.

i don't want to drag you down-
figure out your goals, your needs, desires

and if you are anything like me,
you'll realize

i don't want to feel like this.
i don't want to feel alone.

my feelings matter,
my story is important.

read that again,
to yourself
or whoever needs to hear it.

i promise.

i am finding
life is full of risks.
introduce yourself,
reach out,
step forward,
speak up,
laugh out loud,
explore.

i find that taking these risks
is what gives me life.

he sees me at my lows
as the strongest,
most beautiful person.

he lifts me up
when nobody else can.

wait for him.

i am tired of the war with my mind,
but i am stronger than my anxiety.
i am stronger than my anxiety.

i found someone with similar love languages.
we instinctively love the same.
we love and receive love the same ways.
it's grounded,
it's effortless,
in all the ways i once
pushed away,
pulled.

you'll find resilience in forgiveness,
you'll find resilience in honesty.

opening your heart again,
lowering the fortress.

you play a part in their story.
read that again.
please,
be kind.

i have finally done it,
you are no longer worth my pen.
the force from what you have done
has finally left me alone.

but with that,
comes a blessing and a curse.
i realize the problems now lie
within my own mind
and not with you.
you are not worth my pen.

137

i'd do anything
to tell her that she'll find it-
a love beyond belief.
waking to his ocean eyes
softly caressing her hair
sweet everythings,
every day.
being the center of his world
his beauty
his dream.
she has to be patient.
i would put the tiniest heart on her calendar
and that if she is reading this,
d o n ' t   s e t t l e.

my heart and i talk
late nights and car rides
over setting suns
fields of yellow and white,
lavender.
all she ever talks about
is
y o u.

lists that changed
my perspective,
and
changed my life
♡

<u>gratitude</u>

i have a home
2 parents
a brother
i have myself
nice car ←
nice cellphone ←
four-wheeler ←
traveled to costa rica & bahamas
a lot of people care about me
5 amazing dogs
an wonderful partner
i'm alive

then, cross off the items that
are purely superficial, they don't
contribute to your growth
or support. focus on the people,
experiences, and (importantly)
dogs that you cannot replace.

<u>**what do i need to do to heal?**</u>

read
practice combating intrusive thoughts
forgive those that have wronged me
let go of my expectations of people
read
write
spend time with friends and family
spend time with my dogs
read
declutter my spaces
learn self-care habits that are practical

<u>self-care strategies i can strive for</u>

meditation
listen to music
going outside often
listening to my body when it needs a nap, food, water, or a break
skincare routine
drinking lots of water
reading often
expressing my feelings in that moment instead of bottling it up
journaling
asking others for help
exercise
warm bath
unplug for the day (or a few hours)
light a candle
stretch
treat myself
pay attention to what makes my body and mind feel good
stop putting my energy into arguing
unfollow people that don't give me joy

<u>positive traits about myself</u>

my drive
my communication skills
my heart
selflessness
quick learner
genuine
open-minded
out-going
meticulous
respectful
easy-going
visionary
curious

<u>say it with me now... "i cannot control"</u>

1. what people think of me
2. intrusive/sabotaging thoughts
3. change
4. the past
5. how people treated me

6. rude people
7. if people understand me or not
8. what loved ones think of me
9. how much love i receive
10. the future

11. the passing of time

<u>..."but i can control"</u>

1. how i carry myself
2. learning to love myself, meditate
3. how i respond to change
4. my attitude towards it: lesson learned
5. choosing to let go/forgive
    (even when they don't deserve it)
6. how kind i am
7. my responses to situations
8. time i spend with loved ones
9. how much love i share
10. where i put my energy
    having hope
    being open to opportunities
11. making it count... being present

> seek to work on one thing i can control, and seek to let go of one thing i cannot control

behind the poems

page six

this poem was written with a vision of a quaint living room, with "when it comes to you" and "fenceposts" by cody johnson playing on repeat. how songs can be about love, but songs can also *feel* like love.

i think of a soft and warm partner, to lean on when you need them. he can see that i'm struggling, but he's patient.

pages ten and fifty-five

i think the sky influences our mood and can also reflect how we're feeling. "if it had to be you and me" is reminiscent of the "if the world was ending" or "if you and i were the only two people left on earth" phrases.

could we find love, joy and comfort together? or, will the skies become void of color, dark and dreary? there's time between the poems, then i decide after seeing some of the worst parts of relationships, that if the world was ending, i'd rather be alone than with the person i'm referencing.

page fourteen

one of my best friends and his girlfriend were constantly fighting. he would ask for advice, i'd give it, and he'd ignore it. then he would run into the same issues over and over, asking me for help. it felt like he was never truly listening or valuing my opinion. i struggled with the reality that they would continue to suffer and impact everyone around them.

i had to remind myself that he was just a teenager and those areas of his brain were not fully developed yet; it would continue to be a toxic cycle.

page sixteen

after going through a breakup, or even a "situationship", i find it difficult to exist in their orbit, to exist in a world where i have to pretend that those moments between us carry no meaning.

pages seventeen and nineteen

i had a teacher in high school that meant the world to me. i leaned on them for support, advice. we were friends, even. but i learned a few years after graduating that everything was a lie.

i walked back into the school, as i had a thousand times. i thought about the joy they brought my life, how much they helped me through so many hard times. i felt burdened by the weight of their choices.

at the start of every class, you would look up at a board that displayed what had happened in history, on that particular day. for example, on April 30, 2024 the board might read "Today in History, George Wash-ington was inaugurated as the first President in 1789." the poem plays off of this concept, that today we needed that teacher. everything the teacher represented during that time of my life, is what these kids need... but he ruined it.

page twenty

my all-time favorite movie is The Notebook, which just gives me warm, summertime, young love feelings. some of the key parts of the movie are walt whitman, the white house with blue shutters and having a second chance at a forever love. the two characters for me, feel like wildflowers that dance in the summer breeze and dancing is something that noah and ally often do together.

page twenty-two

i think we all wear a mask, of pretending we are fine but inside, we are deeply hurting. this poem is in response to this idea, where i write to my partner to be more transparent.

also, there's this idea i have, that you cannot feel true love until you experience every version of what love is not. at the same time, you cannot claim to know me and deeply understand me until you see everything that is dark, depressing and lonely.

pages twenty-three and forty-two

i've caused so much collateral damage. i've been hurt so many times before and when this happens, i want the guy to feel just a fraction of what i feel. for example, my first boyfriend cheated and lied the whole relationship. so i cheated back, to hurt him.

do i regret it? absolutely. to save us both the trouble, i should've ended it with the boyfriend as soon as he betrayed me and never looked back.

page twenty-four

"reflections" is simultaneously about the feelings when looking at myself in the mirror and reflecting on my inner thought processes.

standing at the mirror, i'm the most self-critical. my mind is often my enemy. i feel detached from myself, divided, like a medicine cabinet where the mirror is split into multiple sections.

when almy drew the illustration to go along with the poem, i was surprised. it took me a little while to understand it, but to me, it looks like one side is a cracked window and its reflection is a divided window. where it's almost breaking apart into big chunks of glass.

page twenty-eight

sometimes my thoughts are debilitating. my body is frozen and i seem to be quiet, but in reality, my mind is on overdrive. it's like my mind is screaming for help but nothing actually comes out of my mouth. in these moments, i don't ask for help. part of it is not wanting to let anyone in but this isn't helpful and i'll just continue to suffer in silence unless i speak up.

page thirty

i was keeping my feelings to myself, for too long. i literally did exactly as the poem describes, i got out of bed and decided that i needed to share it. what's holding me back?

sharing this, despite some hesitations and vulnerability, will bring me more peace and may help someone else too. i'm not helping anyone by storing it privately to myself.

page thirty-two

the bridge on my family's farm is beautiful. i walk down there to just think and breathe. i reflect a lot, a spot that my ancestors have walked on. the only sounds you can ever hear are the peepers that chirp on summer nights, and the swirl of the stream below.

this poem represents the mixture of emotions- depression, dejection, loneliness, anger, longing... wanting to reinvent yourself.

page thirty-seven

if you have any interest in fantasy, worldbuilding, lovely characters, a complex story line, corruption, magic and romance... the throne of glass series by sarah j. maas is the best. i grew up reading dystopian books like the divergent series but throne of glass really sparked my interest in fantasy and i fell in love with reading again.

i so desperately wanted to find my carranam, a soulmate that would change everything for me. little did i know, i would meet my carranam, jarod.

pages thirty-eight and sixty-two

psa to all of my girlies that have been cheated on, it's likely that your partner started cheating or betraying you, long before the moment you discovered it. they'll claim it was a mistake, but it was only a mistake once you found out, not when they did it multiple times whilst you were unaware.

in the spirit of being transparent, i also admitted in this poem that i was worried i would become the worst version of myself and make the same mistakes that i made in my past. i cheated in my first relationship (see behind the poem, page twenty-three for context) but i regretted it. i don't want to be anything like that person anymore and i certainly do not want to be considered in the same category as my partner's ex. while i cannot control how someone views me, i can control my actions moving forward, to prove that i am never going to make that mistake again.

page thirty-nine

there's a difference between loving someone, being in love with someone and caring about someone. relationships either have all three or they are lacking key pieces. in my previous long-term relationship, i think he loved me but he wasn't in love with me, and he certainly did not truly care about me. he did not value my desires, my needs and my time.

page forty-three

my dad used to tell me how his whole family, my grandparents and their five boys, would pile into the car to go to church every sunday (realistically, the oldest was probably already deployed in the military so maybe only four boys in the car). then, on the way home, my grandfather would drive on the back roads until they got lost, on purpose. part of it was probably to annoy my grandmother, but they also had time to kill.

my papa valued quality time and family time. he and my grandma instilled that in their children and then their children passed those values onto us, the grandchildren.

page forty-four

it doesn't matter if i consented when i was drunk. drunk consent is invalid. if i was sober, i certainly wouldn't have consented. this piece is deeply personal but deserves to be shared and the message cannot be overstated.

page forty-five

i had an imposter syndrome experience, when i starting dating my husband. everything seemed too good to be true and that i didn't deserve him.

memories, regrets, mistakes- it clouded my mind because if he knew that side of me, i thought his feelings would change. but these choices and things i went through don't define who i am and they don't change my worth. i am worthy of love.

page forty-nine

i thought about that experience of losing someone you love and then you start to notice signs that they're watching over you. or, you feel that they are with you, you feel them all around you. you'll see more themes of grief in volume two.

page fifty-six

this piece came straight from within, in a whirlwind of feelings. the subject is feeling like she's trapped in a nightmare, with this guy that has complete control over her. he's all that she thinks about, the memories of them together plague her and haunt her. she's a victim being held hostage and trapped in chains, but ready to fight him and/or kill him, if she gets the chance.

but then her safe haven approaches from behind, able to get close enough to show her true love and grace. he acknowledges her anger but wants to save her from the nightmare. he embraces her and wants her to find peace at the end of this.

page fifty-nine

i feel like many people operate on a fast highway, obsessed with escaping reality... whether it's drinking, gambling, drugs, recklessness. meanwhile, i'm a person that thrives on a dirt road, windows down, not needing much to be happy. i don't want to be like them.

pages sixty-three through sixty-seven

all of these poems were written about a guy i had met a few years ago. it's wild that in just one night you can feel so connected to a person, to want to know everything about them.

at the same time, you're learning to just enjoy the moment because that is the only time you're guaranteed to have with them. i had never felt so deeply intimate with a person before that night, and still so doubtful that it would work. it felt a little like dating stephen demarco from "tell me lies", a charming manipulator. needless to say, the situationship did not last and he ended up ghosting me.

pages seventy-two and ninety-eight

i dated someone on and off for three years. in that time span, he went back and forth on his desire to have children. this was a deal breaker and he knew it. he didn't have any clue what he wanted in that regard, but he was very specific and stubborn about everything else.

i remember driving home from a sushi date and the song "prayed for you" by matt stell came on. i was so excited to tell him about this song and how it reminded me of our love. about thirty seconds in, he was repulsed by the song (likely because it was pop music) and told me to turn it off. that flicked a major switch in my brain, it turned me off... the little things, the attention to my feelings, did not matter to him. he was not my person. i added an epilogue of sorts, to the original poem, which explains itself.

page seventy-three

personifying Fate was a really neat concept to me. i'm a big believer in "everything happens for a reason" but what if a spiritual being named Fate had the ability to see what was in my future? what if she was writing my story and scratched the ending she originally wrote, tore out the pages that were wasted on my ex and smiled at how amazing the next chapter would be.

i think Fate was laughing, putting Jarod into my path. literally the perfect fit and he happened to slide into my dms, the same day i broke up with my ex. the timing couldn't have been crazier.

page seventy-five

when looking back on my previous relationships, i find it very hard to think about the happy times. once it ends, the negative traits, toxicity and pain will consume my memories of them.

sometimes, a happy thought will sneak through the cracks and i lie there wondering if it was all bad, or if my anger and bitterness is just taking over.

page seventy-nine

if i were to personify my heart, it's this abstract, bubbly, hopeless romantic who feels everything. she's messy, with paint on her face and in her hair, the studio has so many meaningful pieces. the landlord, which is also myself, doesn't take care of her, but she doesn't care. she exists and is full of joy, regardless. she bounces back when she is broken.

my mind is this complex, mysterious moon. it seems so far away sometimes, like my mind is difficult to understand. also, i like how we only see the one side of the moon, there's an entire "dark side" of the moon that nobody gets to see.

pages eighty-two and eighty-three

i often describe my mind as this terrible yet fascinating thing- it generates (what feels like) a million thoughts a day, whether it's tearing me down, motivating me, worrying, thinking about the next item on my to-do list or replaying memories. i've also learned that my mind is a product of the environment around it, my past experiences, including relationships that were toxic and my childhood that was riddled with divorce, arguments and perfectionism. my mind only does what it can to survive and adapt to what is happening around me.

pages eighty-eight through ninety

your first relationship, first love, leaves a big impact on your life. my ex emotionally cheated multiple times throughout the relationship, continued to lie, and then used me for months. he told his friends that he wanted to break up with me months prior to when things actually ended, it was greattt. i wish i had realized sooner or had someone wake me up to the fact that i could find someone who would treat me with respect and honesty. ya know, the bare minimum.

i feel like that relationship stole pieces of me that i will never get back, like my innocence, naivety, always seeing the good in someone. i became so paranoid and developed deep trust issues, that affected me for years and still impacts me today. i feel like to some level, i've forgiven him because we were young and both navigating our first relationship but it doesn't erase what he took from me and planted in my mind.

page ninety-two

overtime, from freely giving your heart to another person, you learn to build a fortress. even a tiny one, a guard to separate you from giving everything to that person too soon. don't ever let a partner have that much control over your happiness and well-being. build yourself up first and find someone that will add to your life.

of course, they will become very important to you as you get deeper into the relationship but until then, make sure to protect yourself.

page ninety-three

this is a voicemail that i wished i received from one of my exes, who completely shattered my self-worth, used me, lied to me and ultimately just didn't know how to treat a woman. i forgave him (see the previous page for reference) and i wasn't perfect either, but i wish he gave me this formal apology and confession.

page ninety-six

every time i arrive at my annual vacation in york, maine, i trek down the large rocks that lead to the ocean. the waves crash, it's peaceful and always stirs emotions in me. it's so beautiful there but it's the memories with my amazing family that mean the most to me. my family has been vacationing in the same exact area of york for over fifty years.

i could sit for hours on the rocks just listening to everything around me and soaking in those moments where time slows down.

page ninety-nine

thinking of mental health on a spectrum definitely helped me with processing my emotions and what i was experiencing. everything is temporary and can change from hour to hour, or day to day. i don't need to sit in my thoughts and i don't need to worry about "always feeling this way" because it will ebb and flow.

page one hundred and two

"dear little girl" was written in the framework of motivating myself, playing into sport psychology a little bit and the core memories of playing on my school's soccer team. we named our soccer balls funny names and we were obsessed with eye-black.

it's a letter to my younger self. i used to hesitate and i lacked self confidence. sometimes i don't feel connected to that little girl, but we're truly the same person deep-down. she is still an identity of mine. if i could tell her now to just embrace herself, i would.

page one hundred and four

why not romanticize yourself? hopeless romantics desire love letters (at least i do) so what would you say in a love letter to yourself? i think you should get to a place where you fall in love with yourself, and write something to yourself or your inner child that needs to be loved.

page one hundred and six

while driving, i'm usually thinking about past memories or regrets. i think about the ways i have changed over the years and what's next for me. but i can't fuel change with the shame of my regrets, i need to fuel change by taking action... and i need to move on from the past. if i continue living in the past, i will never reach my destination.

i also need to play music in my car, always, to stop this thought cycle from driving me insane.

pages one hundred and eight and one hundred and twenty

i feel like there comes a time in your relationship that you wonder if they are "your person" or "the one" that you are meant to be with. from my experience, if you have to wonder and question it, that is your sign that they are *not* your person.

i always thought the phrase "when you know, you know" was bullshit until i met Jarod. i knew he was "the one" within a month of dating him. i was acquaintances/classmates with him for over a year, but that feeling is in comparison to a three-year relationship where i still didn't feel confident in being with him for the rest of my life.

I despise the feeling of restlessness, when it comes to being in a relationship with someone. while relationships are not perfect, Jarod brought (and continues to bring) so much peace into my life.

page one hundred and eleven

i want my future children to love themselves but i fear that self-love can only truly be developed through experiences that try to break you. i know that children and teens can grow to love themselves without first picking apart their perceived flaws... but i believe self-love is only at its strongest when it has been tested, time and time again. the most solid form of this can only be built through a journey, a healing process.

pages one hundred and twelve and one hundred and thirteen

my mind spirals when thinking about the past, mistakes i've made, any bad memories. but i can't change what happened back then and i can't change what i did. i can only look forward.

investing in yourself is the most important, long-term project you will ever have. i haven't met anyone who isn't a little broken inside, healing from something. unfortunately that healing is a journey, but that also means that you need to have hope that it will get better, in time.

pages one hundred and sixteen and one hundred and seventeen (one poem)

i really love this piece, it makes me think about writers immortalizing their feelings, who they are, memories and even their lovers. they are permanently putting stories into text whether it's through poetry, a book or a diary. i feel like writers need to let it out and if they don't, the writer feels like they are suffocating from the pressure of their thoughts.

also this poem touches on other feelings, like how one person can greatly impact your life. who are you to the writer? are you their steady partner (their "rock") or are you the villain in their story? the knife refers to betrayal, a knife in the back.

writers bring light to many different human experiences which can help with processing emotions.

page one hundred and eighteen

the subject of this poem is myself, shocker. the subject is thinking about how some emotions and experiences are nicer to think about and feel, rather than dealing with difficult things like heartbreak, learning to love yourself, etc.

i purposefully chose to cut off the end of the poem. i wanted to make it feel like the subject was slowly falling asleep while having these thoughts.

page one hundred and twenty-six

i watch so many people, through my own connections or even on the news, fall into depression, addiction or choose to numb the pain with something. i used to wonder how someone could choose to go down those paths, and even though it can start with choices, it can quickly get out of your control. almost as if you are watching your life spiral right in front of you.

depending on what someone is trying to escape, what pain they are trying to bury, these addictions or thoughts of self-harm can sometimes feel like the only way out of the pain.

we need to lean on our support system or learn how to build one... and end the stigma on both mental health struggles and addiction.

page one hundred and thirty-three

my husband and i have the same love languages and it makes most of our relationship effortless, combined with emotional maturity, respect, honesty. it's not perfect, but in all of the ways i used to push the guy away or demand "more", for him it's easy to provide.

we value (and need in a relationship) what's called "words of affirmation" and because that is true for both of us, communicating our feelings is always the first thing that we give. there were times in the beginning where we thought maybe this was too good to be true, but then we'd both talk about those feelings. our doubts, worries and insecurities slowly faded into the background because we were finally in a relationship where the other person understood who we are and what we need to feel comfortable/secure.

it even got to a point where i questioned if "words of affirmation" was even my primary love language because i felt so confident in the reassurance he gave me, that i felt i didn't "need" it anymore. i realized that i had sought after this level of care and communication in every relationship and never fully received it until now. i'm not saying that this connection of love languages is the secret to everything, or that it's necessary to find a partner that has the same as you... but i am definitely saying that love languages is important.

page one hundred and thirty-eight

a popular question i've seen is "if you could go back and tell your younger self anything, what would you say?" and the fact that i would find the love of my life is a big one. i always wondered growing up if i would find him, or would i always settle for mediocre; that was a fear of mine. especially after the heartache and bullshit i endured, i thought maybe i would have that trajectory forever.

the day on the calendar, i broke off my long-term relationship. i made a big decision for myself that i would rather be single, than wondering everyday if he was the right person for me. i needed to figure out exactly what i wanted and i couldn't do that if were dependent on each other.

little did i know, that hours later, my crush (Jarod) messaged me. we had never talked outside of the college classrooms... i was shocked. the timing was wild. the connection then bloomed into romance and if you had told me this would happen in my future, i would have laughed at you... the right guy is worth the wait.

i hope you saw through the progression of this poetry collection, that i started with some big questions, unknowns, sadness and insecurity and that over time, i ended the collection with more hopeful pieces, a better understanding of who i am, and the best love i could've ever imagined. your journey could be the same. i'm excited for you to see volume two and see how my journey has changed since 2021.

acknowledgments

you, holding the book, that's all i've wanted. so thank you. thank you so much for taking the time to read my story and explore my wonderful mess of a mind. i always knew i would share my writing, but it's a whole different level once it reaches the hands of someone else. i hope at least one poem will stay with you, and be with you in the moments you need it.

this book wouldn't be the dream it is today without the support of my parents when i was "writing books" on the desktop in my purple and gold bedroom. thank you for buying endless amounts of books and reminding me that "you only go this way once."

a special thanks to my friends colleen, bucky, breonna, and almy. lastly, the joy and readiness for my story to be told would not have happened without the love and support from my carranam, jarod. i love you.

about the author

mackenzie was born and raised in upstate, new york. she has always been passionate for the outdoors, reading and writing. mackenzie, a former teacher, now works in higher education and she plans to write young adult fiction in the future. she lives in a cozy home with her husband and two rescue dogs, zoey and skye. this is her debut poetry collection.

questions for the author

why did you choose the title of the book to be *Valleys in my Mind*?

"there's a lot of reasons why it felt right for me. it's one of the earliest poems i wrote. when thinking of a way to describe my mind, that imagery popped up instantly."

"i think my mind is a lot like peaks and valleys. i think the peaks represent all of the exciting moments, the milestones. valleys represent everything else- the quiet moments, the little details, what i hide from others, the shadows and sadness. my mind certainly contains more valleys than peaks, but i'm getting there."

"finally, i love the poem's simplicity and how it represents what i dream about and what brings me peace. almy is an amazing artist and longtime friend of mine; i'm so grateful that she captured it into a cover design and then in the illustration on the first page too."

which piece is your favorite?

"i think 'her spot' is what speaks to me the most. it gives you the best glimpse of what i've experienced. that's the place i walk to and also where i go mentally when i'm in either a creative mood or depressive slump: the bridge to my family's farm. it's so beautiful there."

how do you handle writer's block?

"i usually just take a deep breath and try to remember that there is no pressure on writing a specific way, or to a deadline. i let it pour out of me, and accept rough drafts as rough drafts. very rarely can you perfect your writing on the first try, so i try less to be precise and edit it and instead try to write what feels good at the time. i can just revisit it later."

"i recognized that some of my best writing moods is during nighttime. i also keep my notes section on my phone ready, in case i get a spark for an idea at a random time (which happens often)."

questions for the author (continued)

advice for other writers?

"i was hesitant to call myself a writer growing up. i believe now, that if writing is your way of sharing your heart- you're a writer. if it's through song, you're a musician, etc."

"you never know who you may impact by sharing your experiences, your feelings, your fears. sit down and write. everyone has a story to tell, and i think you should tell yours."

"if you don't feel creative, that's okay. even if you don't feel like you're a good writer, that's okay too. if you don't like what you wrote, sleep on it. go back, think about what you want to illustrate/ create. is there a message you want to leave your audience? did you say everything you wanted to, without holding back?
why do you want to write that piece?
what would you say to someone that hurt you?
what weighs you down?"

"i promise, you are a better writer than you think you are. your story deserves to be shared. i attended a creative writing club in college to be exposed to other writers and that has helped my confidence tremendously."

were there any challenges you faced while writing these poems?

"in the beginning, all i wanted to do hold a physical book of my writing. but then, as i thought about sharing it with others, there's a level of vulnerability involved. i would be stepping over a point of no return. if i was going to share my writing, i had to lose a level of secrecy, privacy and control. i wanted to help people though and show others that they are not alone in these big feelings. that includes letting people in, to a level of knowledge about what i go through."

what are your plans for the future?

"i want to write a lot more. i never thought i was good enough, or that i could possibly do this. now, i'm 22 and i think someday my books will be found on store shelves. there's romance i want to share, visions of characters and stories i want to bring to life. if i continue to believe in myself, you'll see novels in the future."

Copyright © 2021 by Mackenzie Akin

All rights reserved. No part of this publication may be reproduced, distributed, or transmitted in any form or by any means, including photocopying, recording, or other electronic or mechanical methods, without the prior written permission of the publisher, except in the case of brief quotations embodied in critical reviews and certain other noncommercial uses permitted by copyright law.

This is a work of fiction. Any resemblance to actual events or persons, living or dead, is entirely coincidental.

First Edition: Published 2021
Edited: 11.30.2024
Printed on Blurb.com using BookWright
Paperback ISBN: 978-1-7366233-4-3
Hardcover ISBN: 978-1-7366233-5-0

Cover Copyright © 2021 by Almy Bartis
Illustrations Copyright © 2021 by Almy Bartis
Find Almy on Instagram: almycarolann
Find Mackenzie on Instagram: mackenzieakin_

an exclusive look at
volume two...

"Mountains of Change"
Release Date: Winter 2025

one that didn't care enough,
exploited, cheated, lied.
one who wanted control,
left me isolated
red-flag-kinda-guy

the ones who left me empty handed,
parts of me they stole-
but then i met you,
the one who made me whole.

i just seek peace
and the problem is that i can't pin a person,
a memory,
a worry.
i just feel lost and on edge,
constantly running
and never at rest.

what brings me closer and closer
like leading me by hand,
is my love of nature,
books,
my dogs,
my husband,
my closest friends.

but where is she?
where is Peace?

starting over is fucking terrifying.
all of the work i put in,
the passion,
heart,
could now mean nothing.
a small chapter of my story,
that i thought would take up the entire book.
i don't have the pen, to keep writing.
i don't know what's on the next page.
i don't have a plan.
i don't have a vision of what that looks like.

they say time heals all wounds,
but i miss you.
i miss your hugs,
the love i felt in your embrace.

i think time makes grief hurt more
reopening old wounds,
creating uglier scars,
a deeper ache.

the time that has passed
since i heard your voice
breaks my heart.

i hope there is a next life,
no
i need it.
a heaven,
rolling fields of lush green,
overlooked from the peaceful porch.
we share the perfect glass of wine
and i can tell you everything.

i need another lifetime,
where i can see you again
and tell you how much i love you.
i don't think i ever said it enough.
they say time heals all wounds,
but nothing could change how much i miss you.

www.ingramcontent.com/pod-product-compliance
Lightning Source LLC
Chambersburg PA
CBHW051925160426
43198CB00012B/2044